BRAIN GAMES

for Clever Kids®

9 Year Olds

Puzzles and solutions
by Dr Gareth Moore

B.Sc (Hons) M.Phil Ph.D

Illustrations and cover
artwork by Chris Dickason

Designed by Imago Create

BRAIN GAMES for Clever Kids®

9 Year Olds

BUSTER BOOKS

Manufacturer: First published in Great Britain in 2024 by Buster Books, an imprint of Michael O'Mara Books Limited, 9 Lion Yard, Tremadoc Road, London SW4 7NQ
www.mombooks.com

Represented by: Authorised Rep Compliance Ltd, Ground Floor, 71 Lower Baggot Street, Dublin D02 P593, Ireland
www.arccompliance.com

 www.mombooks.com/buster   Buster Books   @buster_books

Clever Kids is a trade mark of Michael O'Mara Books Limited.

Puzzles and solutions © Gareth Moore

Illustrations and layouts © Buster Books 2024

A CIP catalogue record for this book is available from the British Library.

ISBN: 978-1-78055-939-1

3 5 7 9 10 8 6 4 2

This product is made of material from well-managed, FSC®-certified forests and other controlled sources. The manufacturing processes conform to the environmental regulations of the country of origin.

Printed and bound in February 2025 by
CPI Group (UK) Ltd, Croydon, CR0 4YY.

For further information see www.mombooks.com/about/sustainability-climate-focus
Report any safety issues to product.safety@mombooks.com

INTRODUCTION

Get ready to push your brain to the limit with these fun-filled games!

Take your pick of 101 puzzles. You can complete them in any order you like and work through at your own pace.

Start each puzzle by reading the instructions. Sometimes this is the hardest part of the puzzle, so don't worry if you have to read the instructions a few times to be clear on what they mean.

Once you know what to do, it's time to battle your way to the answer. Time yourself completing each puzzle, and write your time in the box at the top of each page. For an extra challenge, you can come back to the puzzles at a later date and see if you can complete them even faster.

There's a notes and scribbles section at the back that you can use to help you work out the answers.

If you really struggle with a puzzle, take a look at the solutions at the back to see how it works, then try it again later and see if you can work it out the second time round.

Good luck, and have fun!

Introducing the Brain Games Master:
Gareth Moore, B.Sc (Hons) M.Phil Ph.D

Dr Gareth Moore is a brain games genius, and author of lots of puzzle books.

He created an online brain-training site called BrainedUp.com, and runs a puzzle site called PuzzleMix.com. Gareth has a Ph.D from the University of Cambridge, where he taught machines to understand spoken English.

Let the BRAIN GAMES begin!

A family have three children: Ally, Bex and Charlie. You also know that:

- Ally is one-third of Bex's age

- In four years' time, Ally will be the same age that Charlie is now

- Charlie is two years younger than Bex

- The oldest child is nine years old

Given the above, which one of the following statements could be true?

a) Ally is 5

b) Bex is 6

c) Charlie is 7

d) Ally is 1

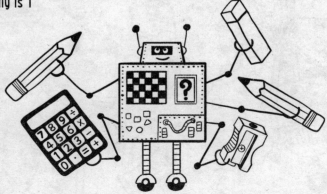

The answer is: ....

Take a look at the vehicle at the top of the page, then at each of the six possible silhouettes below. Which of these silhouettes exactly matches the outline of the car?

a)   b)   c)

d)   e)   f)

The answer is: ....

Can you circle the ten differences between these two images?

In each number pyramid on these pages, every block should contain a value equal to the result of adding together the two numbers directly beneath it. Can you fill in all the empty blocks to follow this rule? You will need to both add and subtract to work them all out.

Here's an example to show what a complete pyramid looks like:

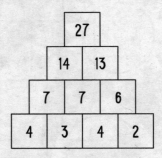

		27		
	14		13	
	7	7	6	
4	3	4	2	

a)

b)

	12

| 5 | 5 | |

| | 2 | |

c)

| 6 | 5 | 6 | 5 |

How quickly can you find your way through this maze, all the way from top to bottom?

Start ⬇

Finish

Lottie, Jack and Mina are each going on holiday to a different place, and are each using a different type of transport to get there. You know that:

- One of the people is travelling by car

- Lottie is going to France

- Someone is going to Canada by plane

- Mina is travelling by boat

- Someone is travelling to Australia

Given the information above, now work out:

a) What type of vehicle is Lottie travelling in? ....

b) Where is Jack going on holiday? ....

c) Which person is going to Australia? ....

You can use the table below to help you keep track of your working:

Person	Country	Transport

Take a look at the aliens opposite, and answer the following questions as quickly as you can – then check more slowly to see if you were correct.

a) How many aliens have all of their eyes fully open?

....

b) How many aliens have exactly 2 antennae and are sticking their tongues out?

....

c) How many aliens are winking but *not* sticking out their tongue?

....

d) Which are there more of: aliens with 3 antennae, or aliens who have two open eyes looking away from the centre of the book?

....

e) How many aliens have only one eye *and* are sticking their tongues out?

....

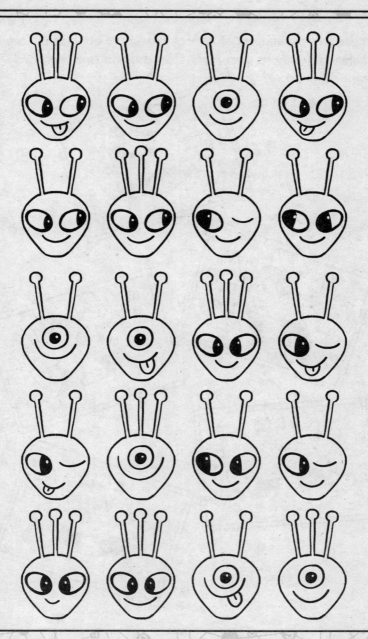

These five pictures might all look the same, but one is slightly different to the others. Can you find and then circle the odd-one-out?

Can you draw along some of the dashed lines to divide this shape up into four identical pieces, with no unused parts left over? Each of the four pieces must be identical, although they can be rotated relative to one another.

Take a look at the solved example, to see how it works.

Each of these two pictures shows the same background image, but in each case different parts of it are covered by white squares.

By imagining combining the two pictures, so the empty squares on one are replaced with the corresponding squares from the other picture, can you say how many circles there would be in the combined image?

The answer is: ....

Take a good look at the six pictures on this page. Once you think you will remember what they are, turn the page and then circle the three new pictures that have been added.

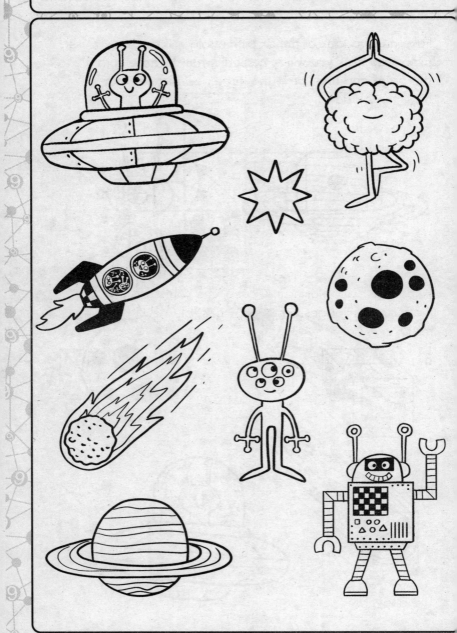

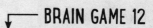

Imagine that you cut out and then fold up the following picture to make a cube with six different faces:

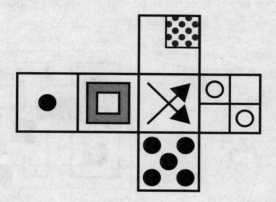

Without actually making the cube, can you say which of the following images would be a possible view of the resulting cube?

a)
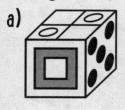

c)

b)

d)

e)
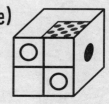

The answer is: ....

Draw lines to make a loop which visits every white square, just like in the example solution below. The loop can't visit any square more than once, or visit a shaded square. This also means that it can't cross itself.

Here's an example solved puzzle, so you can see how it works:

a)

b)

c)

Can you find each of these fourteen numbers in the grid?
They can be written in any direction, including diagonally,
and may read forwards or backwards.

124111	409434	710080	987611
224165	457207	73417	994098
269984	558212	896759	
369864	56248	957590	

2	5	9	2	1	4	6	8	9	6	3	9
4	5	1	0	7	4	6	9	2	4	5	9
9	8	9	1	6	1	2	4	5	9	9	4
2	2	2	2	2	6	0	7	0	5	9	0
5	1	1	2	9	4	2	0	7	0	5	9
6	2	4	9	4	0	1	6	8	2	7	8
6	4	8	0	7	1	9	1	1	0	5	5
8	4	2	6	9	8	6	1	1	6	9	7
4	4	8	5	1	4	6	5	7	1	0	1
8	2	2	0	5	7	3	3	5	1	0	4
6	1	5	6	8	0	9	4	6	7	8	3
1	9	4	9	5	1	9	2	9	1	9	7

Can you help complete this jigsaw puzzle by finding the four pieces that are required, and drawing lines to show where they fit? Unfortunately the pieces have been mixed up with two more from a different puzzle.

Some fish are hiding in each of these ponds. Can you find them all?

- None of the fish are in the grid squares with numbers on.

- There is never more than one fish per grid square.

- Numbers reveal the total number of fish in all touching squares – including diagonally touching squares.

Look at this solved puzzle to see how this works:

a)

b)

	3		1
	4	2	
1			1

c)

	1		3	
2	2			
		2	2	
1	2			1

Write a digit from 1 to 6 into each empty square so that no digit repeats in any row, column or bold-lined 3x2 box.

Here's an example solved puzzle, to show how it works:

1	2	4	5	3	6
3	5	6	1	2	4
5	1	3	6	4	2
6	4	2	3	1	5
2	3	5	4	6	1
4	6	1	2	5	3

a)

	4	2	3	6	
3		5	2		4
5	1			2	6
6	2			5	3
4		1	6		2
	3	6	5	4	

b)

6					5
		1	2		
	1			2	
	6			5	
		6	3		
2					6

c)

3					6
	2			4	
		5	4		
		1	2		
	4			5	
1					4

Draw horizontal and vertical lines to join all the dots into a single loop, which doesn't revisit any dot. Some of the dots are joined already to get you started.

Here's an example solved puzzle to show you how it works:

a)

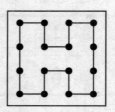

b)

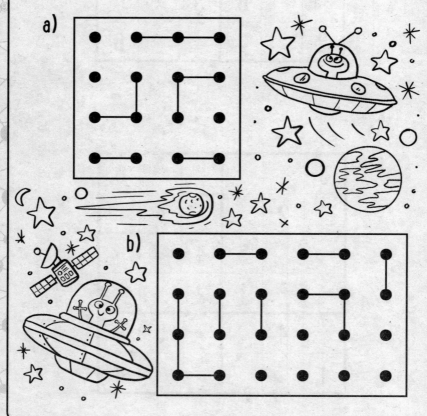

c)

d)

Draw along the dashed lines to divide the grid up into four regions, so that each region contains exactly one of each letter from A to D.

Take a look at this example solved puzzle to see how this works:

a)

A	C	C	A
C	D	B	D
B	C	D	B
D	A	B	A

TIME ....

b)

B	D	A	D
B	A	C	B
C	D	C	A
A	C	B	D

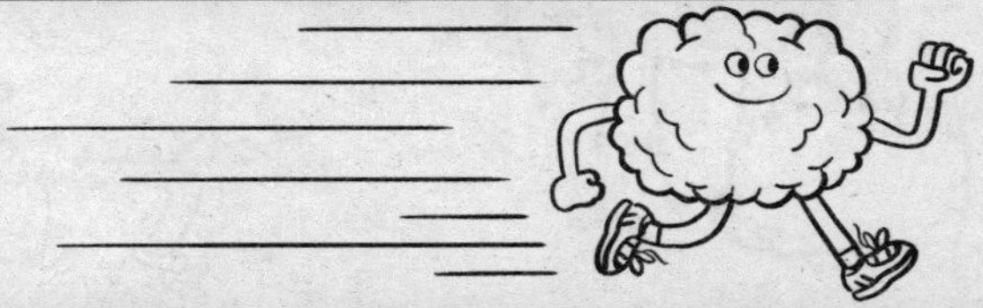

c)

A	D	D	C	A
C	C	A	B	B
D	B	D	A	C
D	B	A	C	B

Draw lines to join each pair of identical shapes, just like in the example solution below. Only one line can enter each square, and lines can't be drawn diagonally.

Here's an example solved puzzle, so you can see how it works:

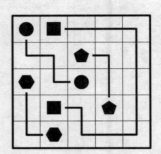

a)

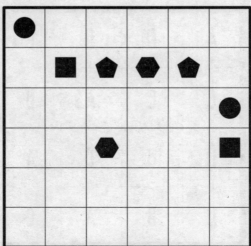

b)

c)

Imagine rotating each of these shapes as shown by the arrow beneath it: 90° clockwise, 180°, and 90° anticlockwise as shown. Which of the options, 1 to 3, will result for each?

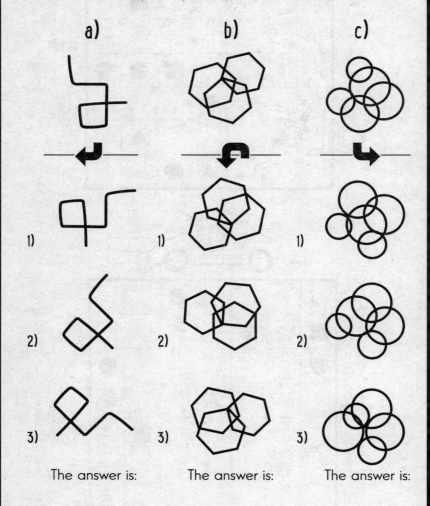

a)

b)

c)

1)

2)

3)

The answer is: The answer is: The answer is:

....

Take a good look at the five aliens on this page. Once you think you will remember what they look like, turn the page.

Two of the aliens have left and been replaced by two new aliens. Circle the two new aliens.

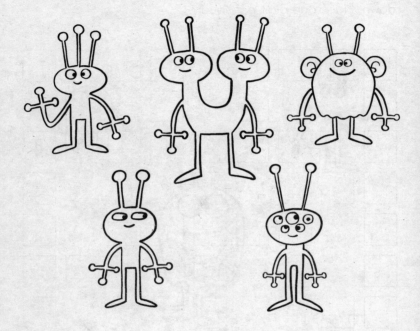

Circle the two aliens who left, choosing from the options below:

TIME ....

BRAIN GAME 23

Place all of the given numbers into the grid, crossword-style, so that each number can be read once either across or down. Place one digit per square.

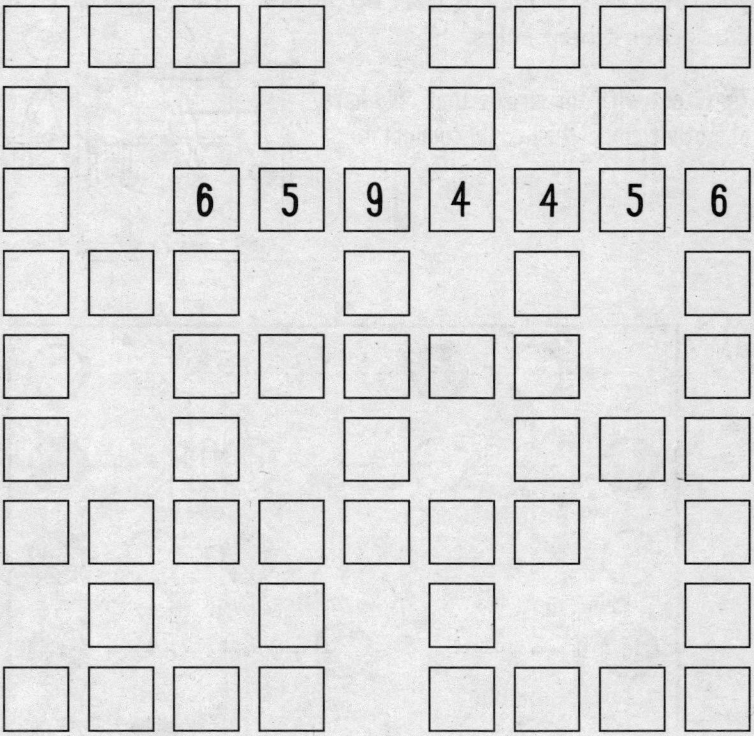

3 Digits		4 Digits	5 Digits	7 Digits
114	625	2471	14793	2943437
135	674	4647	42339	~~6594456~~
312	794	7163	62193	6619297
389	982	9422	98778	7639819

Draw over some of the dashed lines to join the circles into pairs. Every pair must contain one shaded circle and one white circle, just like in the example solution below. Every circle must be part of a pair of exactly two circles. The lines you draw must not cross over each other. They also can't cross over other circles.

Tip: Start with the circles that only have one other circle they could connect to.

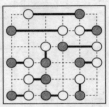

a)

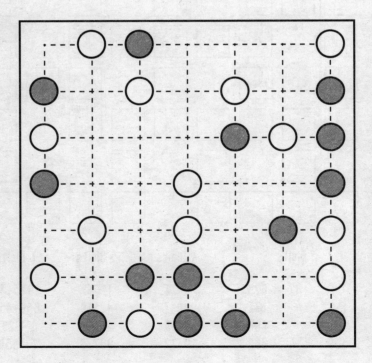

b)

First, find the most direct route all the way from the top to the bottom of this maze. Then, what is the total value of all the numbers that the route passes through?

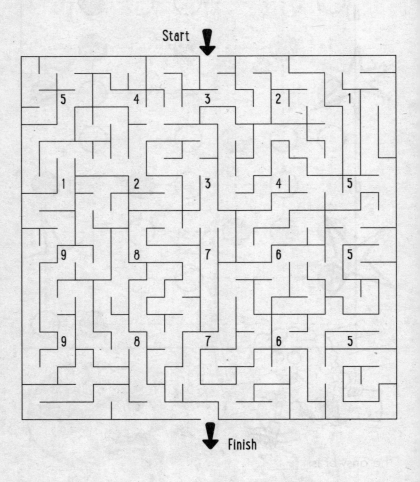

The answer is: ....

One of the following images is not like the others. Which one, and why?

a)

b)

c)

d)

e)

f)

The answer is: ....

....

Write a letter from 'A' to 'F' into each empty square so that
no letter repeats in any row or column. Also, identical letters
cannot be in touching squares – not even diagonally.

Here's an example solved puzzle,
so you can see how it works:

C	F	D	B	E	A
E	B	A	C	D	F
D	C	F	E	A	B
A	E	B	D	F	C
F	D	C	A	B	E
B	A	E	F	C	D

a)

B		A	E		C
		C	B		
E	B			C	A
D	C			B	F
		B	C		
C		F	D		B

b)

		B	E		
D		F	B		A
B		A	D		F
		E	A		

The time in New York City is five hours behind the time in London. That means that when it is 10am in London, it is 5am in New York City.

a) If the time is currently 8pm in London, what time is it in New York City?

....

b) If the time is now 11am in New York City, what time is it in London?

....

The time in Los Angeles is three hours behind the time in New York City, so when it is 5am in New York City it is 2am in Los Angeles.

c) If it's now 3pm in Los Angeles, what time is it in New York City?

....

d) If it's midnight in London, what time is it in Los Angeles?

....

These six pictures look similar, but in fact only two of them are identical. All the others have a small difference compared to the rest. Can you draw a line to join the identical pair, then circle the difference on each of the other pictures?

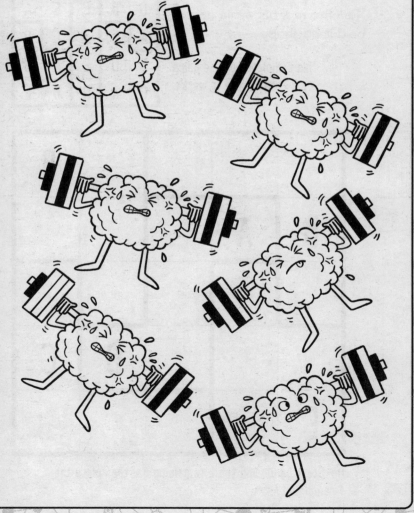

Complete each of these jigdoku puzzles by placing a letter from 'A' to 'E' into each empty square. Place letters so that:

- No letter repeats in any row or column

- No letter repeats within any bold-lined shape

This completed puzzle helps show how it works:

E	C	A	D	B
D	B	C	E	A
A	E	B	C	D
B	D	E	A	C
C	A	D	B	E

a)

				B
B	A			
			B	C
E				

Tip: Start by placing the 2 remaining 'B's, then place the 4 remaining 'A's.

b)

Tip: Start by placing the 3 remaining 'C's. then place the 3 remaining 'E's.

Imagine folding a square of paper in half twice, then cutting out an arrow as shown.

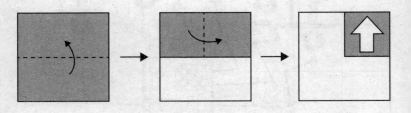

If you now fully unfold the paper, which of the following will result?

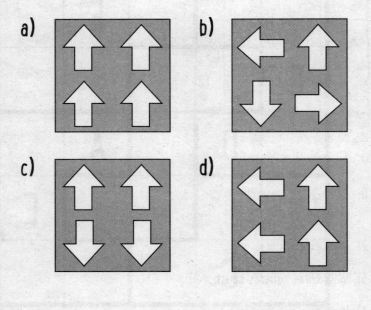

a)

b)

c)

d)

The answer is: ....

Take a look at this map, which has been overlaid with a grid. To the right of it is a compass, showing which way is north, east, south and west.

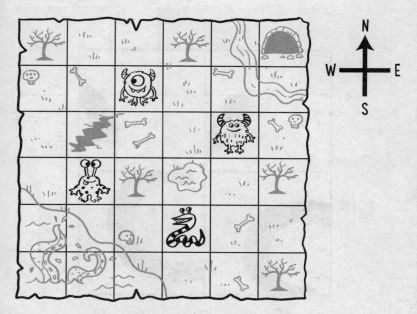

You go for a walk as described below. Draw your route, and circle the monster where you end up.

1) Start at the location of the most northerly monster

2) Walk two squares west

3) Walk three squares south

4) Walk two squares east

5) Walk one square south

6) Walk three squares east

7) Walk five squares north

8) Walk one square west

9) Walk two squares south

⏰ TIME ....

These four tiles can be swapped around to reveal a picture of a number. What is that number? You don't need to rotate any of the tiles.

The answer is: ....

Imagine looking down on this arrangement of cubes from the direction of the arrow. Which of the options, A to D, would match what you see?

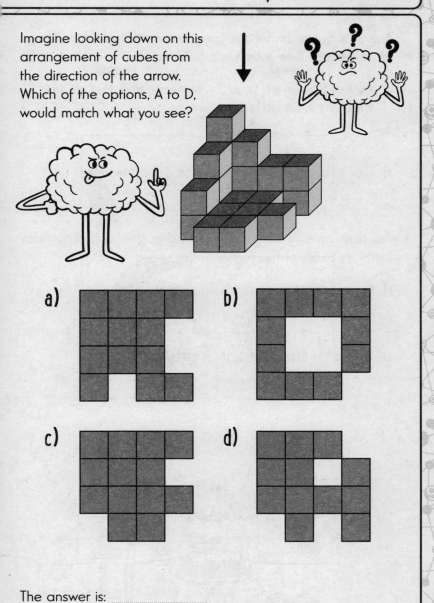

a)

b)

c)

d)

The answer is: ....

⏱ TIME ....

Anisha is going on holiday for a week with her family. They leave on 10th June, which is a Saturday.

a) Anisha's birthday will be on the Wednesday while they are away. What date is her birthday on?

....

b) Their holiday ends on 18th June. What day of the week is this?

....

Ten days after Anisha's actual birthday, she hosts a birthday party for some of her friends.

c) On what day of the week is Anisha's birthday party?

....

d) What is the date of her birthday party?

....

How many rectangles, of various sizes, can you count in the following picture? Don't forget the large one all around the outside!

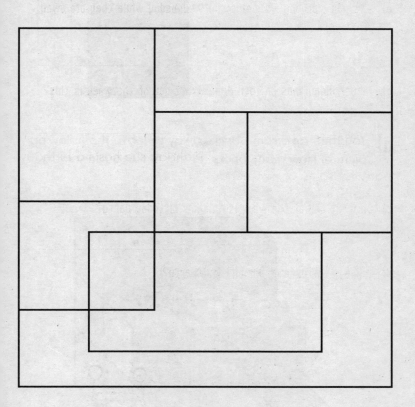

Imagine that you have arranged
27 bricks to form a 3x3x3 cube,
so they look like this:

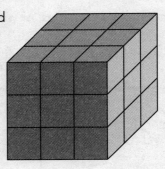

a) You then take some bricks away to leave the following
picture. How many bricks remain in this arrangement?

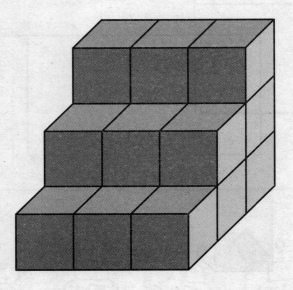

The answer is: ....

b) You then put all the bricks back so there are 27 of them again. Now you remove some more again to leave the following arrangement. How many bricks are left this time?

The answer is: ....

Can you draw either an 'X' or an 'O' into every empty box of each puzzle so that no lines of four 'X's or 'O's in a row are formed?

Here's an example solved puzzle, so you can see how it works:

a)

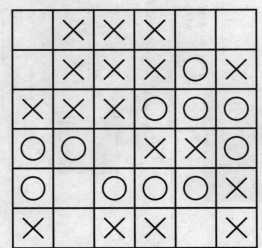

b)

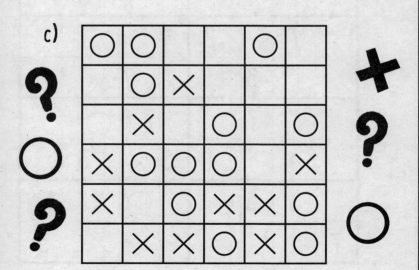

c)

Write a digit from 1 to 8 into each empty square so that no digit repeats in any row, column or bold-lined 4x2 box.

Here's an example solved puzzle:

3	2	4	8	7	5	1	6
7	1	5	6	2	4	3	8
1	7	2	3	8	6	4	5
8	5	6	4	1	3	2	7
2	6	3	7	5	1	8	4
4	8	1	5	6	2	7	3
5	4	8	2	3	7	6	1
6	3	7	1	4	8	5	2

a)

8							5
	2	1			6	8	
	7		2	4		1	
		3			7		
		7			8		
	4		1	5		3	
	3	5			4	7	
7							3

b)

		7	3	5	1		
	2	3	8	6	5	4	
	7	5			2	8	
	3	8			6	5	
	5	4	6	7	8	1	
		6	2	1	7		

Draw along the dashed lines to create fences that divide each of these grids into a set of square fields, just like in the example below. Every field must contain exactly one monster, and every grid square must be part of exactly one field.

Take a look at this example to see how this works:

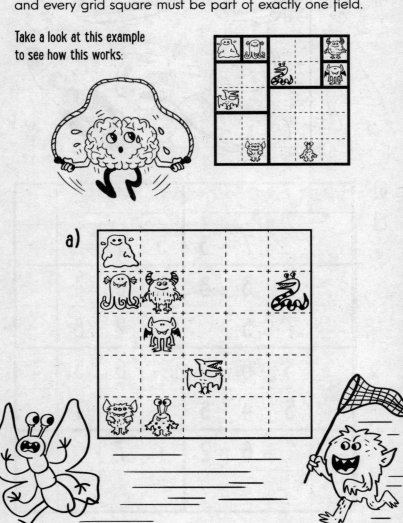

a)

b)

c)

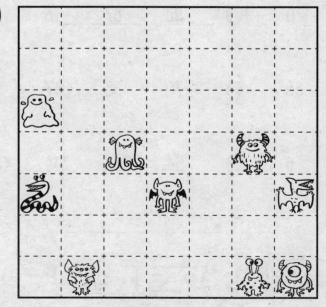

Cross out one number in each of the following rows to create a mathematical number sequence. For example, if the numbers were 2 4 6 7 8 10 then you could cross out the 7 to leave 2 4 6 8 10, creating the sequence 'add 2 at each step'.

a) 4   7   9   10   13   16

b) 88   66   44   22   11   5½

c) 120   109   98   87   76   67

d) 58   63   70   78   87   97

e) 6   18   54   162   314   486

Take a good look at the five monsters on this page. Once you think you will remember what they look like, turn the page.

Two of the monsters have left and been replaced by two new ones. Circle the two new monsters.

Now circle the two monsters who left, choosing from the options below:

Join all of the following numbers into pairs, so that one is exactly twice the value of the other. Each number can be in only one pair. Be careful because there are multiple ways to make some of the pairs, but only one way to place them all into pairs at the same time.

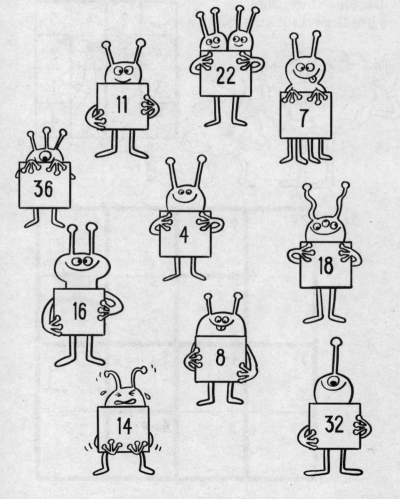

Place a number from 1 to 4 into each square so that no number you place repeats in any row or column. The numbers inside each bold-lined area must add up to make the small number printed at the top-left of that area.

Take a look at this solved puzzle to see how it works:

1	3+	10+	
1	2	4	3
7+	1	3	3+
4	1	3	2
3	9+	3+	
3	4	2	1
2	3	1	4
			4

a)

7+	4	3+	4+
	2		
3+	4+	3	6+
		4	

b)

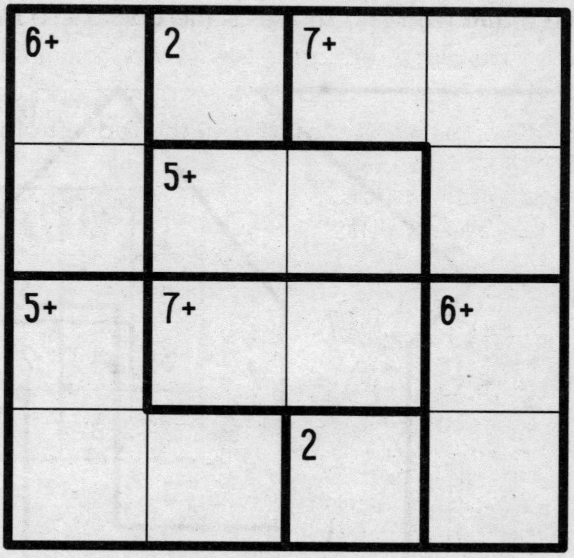

6+	2	7+	
	5+		
5+	7+		6+
		2	

c)

4+		6+	
7+	4+		3+
	6+		
6+		4+	

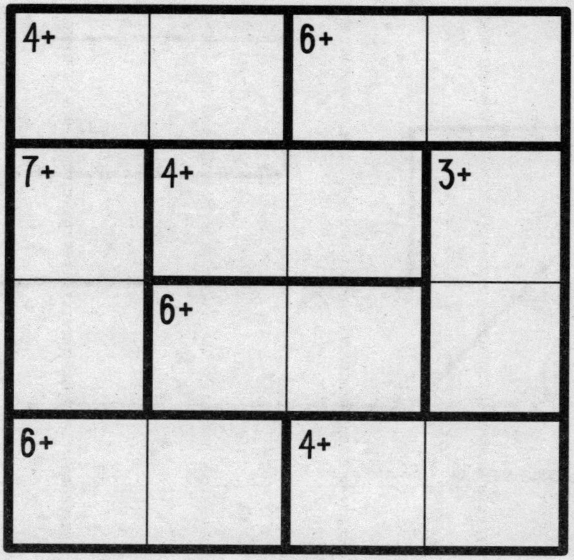

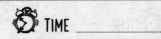

Which of the following shapes is the odd one out, and why?

a)

b)

c)

d)

The answer is:

One of the following numbers doesn't fit in with the rest. Can you work out which is this odd one out, and say why?

The answer is: ....

....

Write a letter from 'A' to 'G' into each empty square so that no letter repeats in any row or column. Also, identical letters cannot be in touching squares – not even diagonally.

Take a look at this solved puzzle to see how it works:

C	D	E	F	B	G	A
B	F	G	A	E	D	C
D	A	C	B	G	F	E
E	G	F	D	C	A	B
A	C	B	G	F	E	D
F	E	A	C	D	B	G
G	B	D	E	A	C	F

a)

	F	E		G	A	
	D	G	F	B		E
		B		D		
	A	F	E	C	B	
	E	C		A	G	

b)

		B		G		
	C				D	
A		E	B	F		C
		F		D		
C		D	E	B		G
	F				E	
		A		C		

Starting from the location marked with an 'X', at which square do you end up if you trace the following route?

←↓←←←↓↓↓→↓→→↑↑↑→↑←←↓←↑

Each arrow indicates you move in the direction shown from one square to the next.

					X

Take a look at this picture, until you think you will remember it. Then, once you are ready, turn the page and redraw it as well as you can.

When you're finished, turn back and see how you did.

How quickly can you find your way through this maze, all the way from top to bottom?

Start ⬇

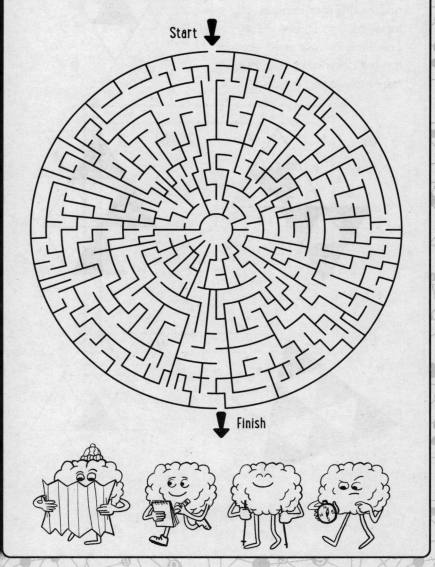

Finish

The image at the top of the page has been hidden in one of the four images labelled A to D, but which one? The answer must contain the full original image, but it may have been rotated.

a)

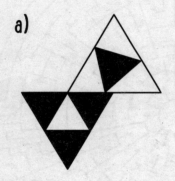

b)

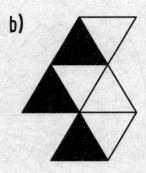

c)

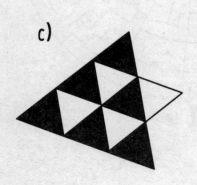

d)

The answer is: ....

Cross out exactly one digit in each of the following incorrect calculations so that they become correct. For example, 12 + 3 = 4 would be correct if you crossed out the '2' so it read 1 + 3 = 4

5 + 16 = 11

10 + 21 = 22

11 × 12 = 22

21 + 10 + 5 = 26

11 + 22 + 33 = 56

Complete each of these jigdoku puzzles by placing a letter from 'A' to 'F' into each empty square. Place letters so that:

- No letter repeats in any row or column

- No letter repeats within any bold-lined shape

This completed puzzle helps show how it works:

D	F	C	A	B	E
C	B	A	E	D	F
F	A	B	D	E	C
A	E	D	F	C	B
B	D	E	C	F	A
E	C	F	B	A	D

a)

F		B		A	D
	D			B	
A		D	F		
	C	D			F
	B			F	
E	F		B		C

Tip: Start by placing the remaining 'F', then the remaining 'C's.

b)

Tip: Start by completing the four empty squares in this bold-lined shape.

Take a look at the group of robots at the top of the page, then at each of the six silhouettes beneath. Can you circle the one silhouette which exactly matches the outline of the robots?

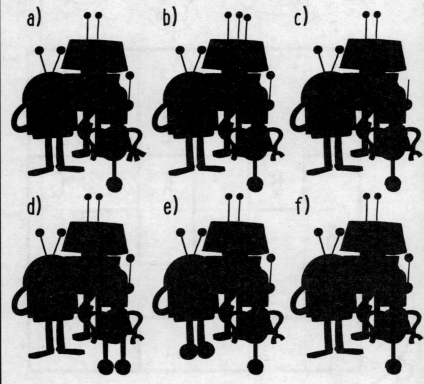

a)

b)

c)

d)

e)

f)

Can you help complete this jigsaw puzzle by finding the four pieces that are required, and drawing lines to show where they fit? Unfortunately the pieces have been mixed up with some from a different puzzle.

Write a number into each empty square so that every number from 1 to 16 appears once in the grid. Numbers must be placed so that they form a path from 1 to 16, stepping left/right/up/down from square to square.

Take a look at this solved puzzle to see how it works:

12	13	14	15
11	10	9	16
6	7	8	1
5	4	3	2

a)

	10		4
		6	3
	8		
			1

TIME ....

b)

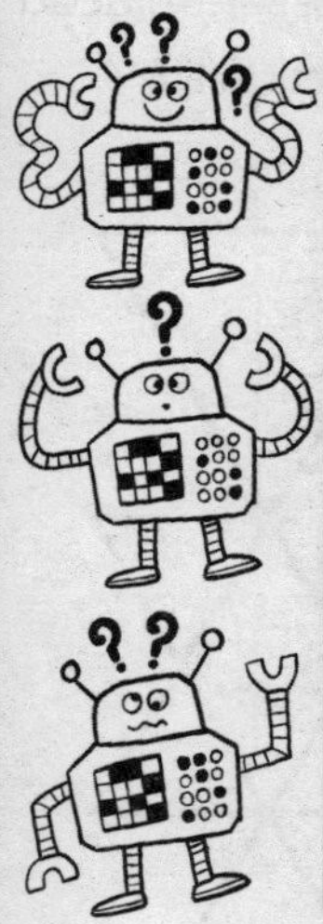

14		12	11
	1		
3			6

c)

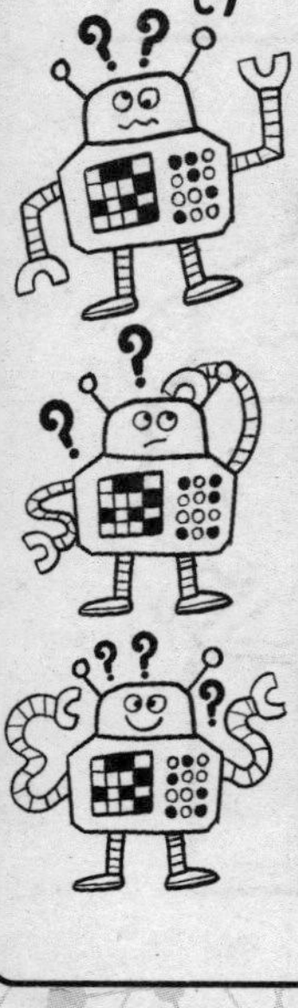

9	10		
		12	
5			14
		2	

Take a look at the picture below, which has been drawn using just triangles. What is the minimum number of triangles you would need to draw to recreate this picture yourself?

.... triangles

Starting on a circle which contains a 1, can you trace a route along the lines to 2, 3, 4, 5 and then 6 in that order, without visiting any number more than once?

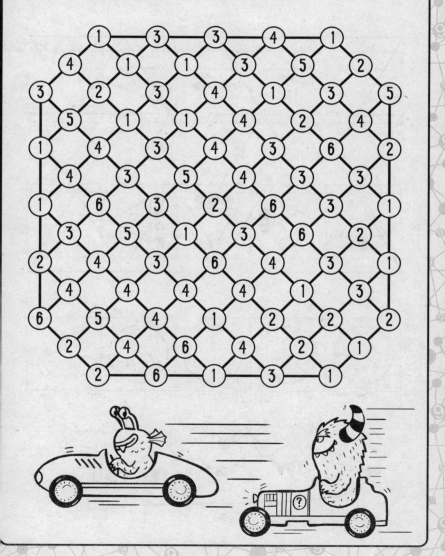

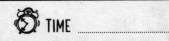

Study each of the sequences below, then draw what should come next in the empty box to the right of each row.

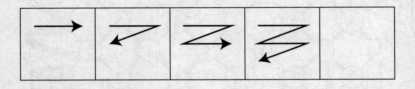

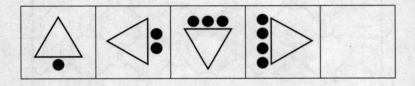

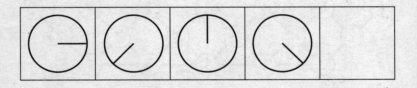

Take a good look at this picture, then when you think you will remember it turn the page.

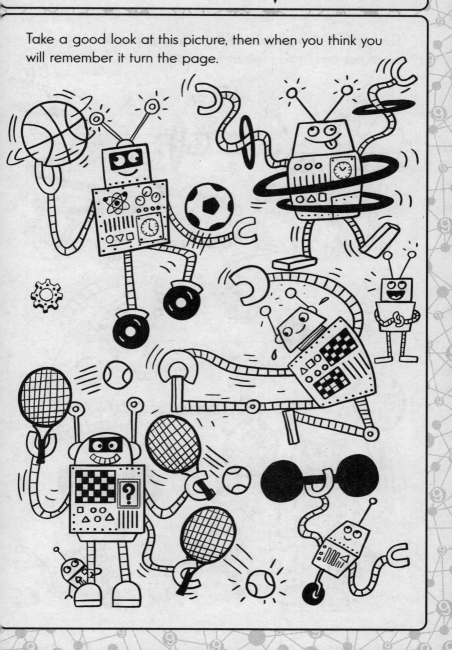

Circle the four changes to the picture. If you can't find them all, check back and forth until you do.

One of the following images is not like the others.
Which one, and why?

a)

b)

c)

d)

e)

f)

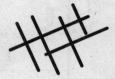

The answer is: ....

....

Write a digit from 1 to 9 into each empty square so that no digit repeats in any row, column or bold-lined 3x3 box.

a)

6		7		8		1		2
	3		7		5		6	
5		4		9		8		7
	1		9		8		2	
4		2		5		9		1
	5		2		4		7	
2		3		6		7		5
	4		8		7		9	
7		9		4		3		8

b)

4		8		6		3		9
		1		9		4		
3	7	9				6	5	2
			9		8			
8	9						2	3
			7		3			
9	8	4				5	7	6
		3		7		8		
6		7		8		2		1

Can you find the twelve differences between these two images?

Place all of the given numbers into the grid, crossword-style, so that each number can be read once either across or down. Place one digit per square.

| 7 | 8 | 9 |

| | | | | 3 Digits | | | 4 Digits | 5 Digits | 7 Digits |

126	573	758	5212	44719	6739525
184	653	789	7632	93597	9149644
393	666	815	8681		
423	671	834	8765		
544	696				

Take a good look at these seven animals. Once you think you will remember them, turn the page and read the instruction.

Two of the animals have now left. Can you say what they were?

Animal 1: ....

Animal 2: ....

Can you find each of these sixteen numbers in the grid?
They can be written in any direction, including diagonally,
and may read forwards or backwards.

233823	632551	739995	874015
326925	659176	750925	926071
525065	681313	837525	94587
571868	689223	848037	977805

7	3	0	8	4	8	3	6	6	0	9	5	7	1
8	7	2	3	2	3	5	3	6	2	3	2	9	1
5	2	5	0	6	5	2	3	6	2	5	5	9	4
8	7	1	7	7	6	2	0	8	3	1	7	4	6
6	6	1	6	9	5	7	3	5	7	8	3	5	7
5	8	7	2	5	1	3	9	0	8	5	8	8	7
1	8	5	1	7	2	0	2	8	6	3	7	7	2
6	8	6	8	1	7	5	6	5	3	6	4	5	4
5	6	6	1	5	5	5	2	2	8	8	8	4	0
0	3	8	5	3	9	1	9	5	2	9	0	5	7
8	9	1	1	1	8	9	0	9	9	2	8	0	5
7	9	2	7	3	8	6	9	4	8	2	7	0	6
7	6	6	5	7	1	1	5	3	7	3	5	7	3
9	6	3	6	5	7	3	1	9	7	8	9	5	7

Place a number from 1 to 4 into each square so that no number you place repeats in any row or column. The numbers inside each bold-lined area must multiply together to make the small number printed at the top-left of that area.

Take a look at this solved puzzle to see how it works:

2× 1	2	12× 3	4
6× 2	4× 1	4	3× 3
3	8× 4	2	1
12× 4	3	2× 1	2

a)

3×	4	2×	
	3×	8×	4
2			3×
8×		3	

TIME ....

b)

2	72×		4×
		1	
4×	1	48×	
			3

c)

12×		8×	
	6×		
8×			36×
2×			

Rashid has a bag of toy balls, which has three different types of ball inside. All the balls are the same size and feel the same. It contains:

- Four red balls

- Eight yellow balls

- Twelve orange balls

Rashid reaches into the bag and pulls out a ball at random, without looking. Which *one* of the following statements is true?

a) Rashid is twice as likely to pull out an orange ball as a yellow ball

b) Rashid is most likely to pull out a yellow ball

c) Rashid is three times as likely to pull out a yellow ball as a red ball

d) Rashid is three times as likely to pull out an orange ball as a red ball

The answer is: ....

How many rectangles, of various sizes, can you count in the following picture? Don't forget the large one all around the outside!

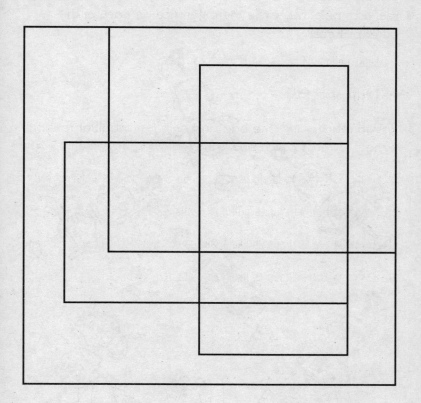

These seven pictures look similar, but in fact only two of them are identical. All the others have a small difference compared to the rest. Can you draw a path to join the identical pair, then circle the difference on each of the other pictures?

Can you complete each of these three number-chain puzzles? Start with the number at the top of each column, then apply each mathematical operation in turn until you reach the bottom of the column. Try to do all of the calculations in your head, without making any written notes.

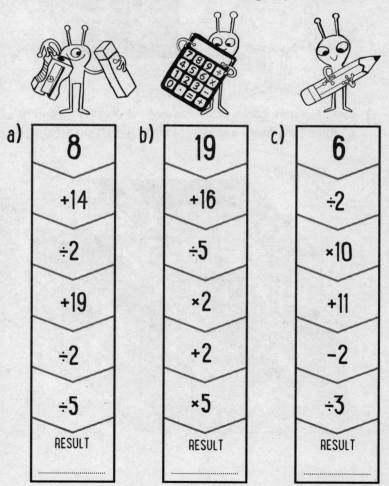

a)

8

+14

÷2

+19

÷2

÷5

RESULT

....

b)

19

+16

÷5

×2

+2

×5

RESULT

....

c)

6

÷2

×10

+11

−2

÷3

RESULT

....

Imagine that you have arranged
64 bricks to form a 4x4x4 cube,
so they look like this:

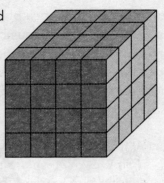

a) You then take some bricks away to leave the following
picture. How many bricks remain in this arrangement?

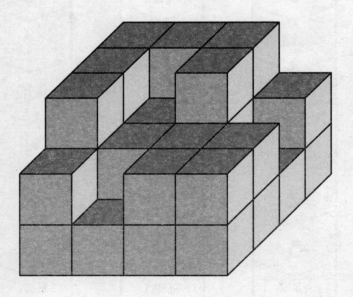

The answer is: ....

b) You then put all the bricks back so there are 64 of them again. Now you remove some more again to leave the following arrangement. How many bricks are left this time?

The answer is: ....

Imagine folding this piece of paper in half twice, then cutting out an arrow and circle as shown.

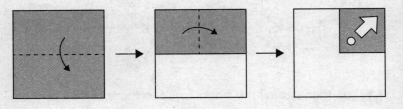

If you now fully unfold the paper, which of the following will result?

a)

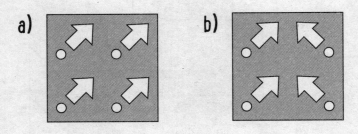

b)

c)

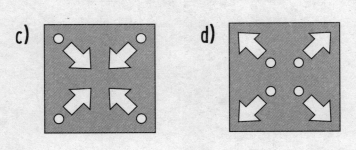

d)

The answer is: ....

Which of the following shapes is the odd one out, and why?

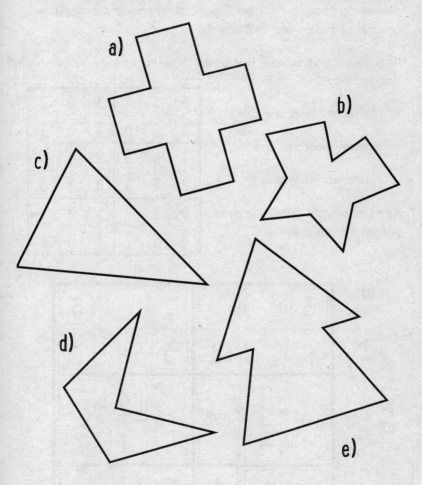

a)

b)

c)

d)

e)

The answer is: ....

....

Write a digit from 1 to 6 into each grid square which does not already contain a digit, so that no digit repeats in any row, column or bold-lined 3x2 box.

Also, every grid square has been labelled to show what values can fit into it:

- No shape: contains 1 or 2

- Square: contains 3 or 4

- Circle: contains 5 or 6

Here's an example solved puzzle, so you can see how it works:

a)

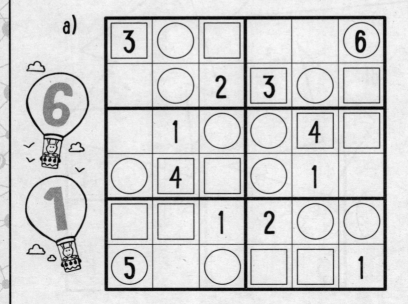

b)

5

3

	○		○	□	□
□	□	⑤	2		○
○	⑤	2	3	4	
	4	3	⑥	⑤	
○		⑥	4		□
□		□		○	○

c)

4

2

2	□	○	○		4
○	□			□	○
□	○	□	○		
	○		□	○	□
○		○	□	□	
3		□		○	⑥

In each number pyramid on these pages, every block should contain a value equal to the result of adding together the two numbers directly beneath it. Can you fill in all the empty blocks to follow this rule? You will need to both add and subtract to work them all out.

Here's an example solved puzzle, to show how it works:

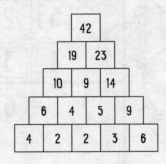

a)

b)

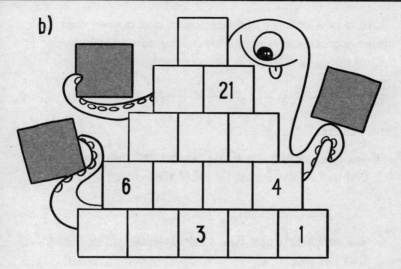

c)

Take a look at the robots opposite, and answer the following questions as quickly as you can – then check more slowly to see if you were correct.

a) How many robots are standing on at least one wheel?

....

b) How many hands do the robots have in total? Their hands are the C-shaped attachments at the end of their curved arms.

....

c) How many robots have two or more antennae *and* are looking away from this page?

....

d) Are there more flat feet or wheels in total?

....

e) How many robots have two or more straight legs *and* also three or more curved arms?

....

f) How many robots are looking towards *their* right?

....

TIME ....

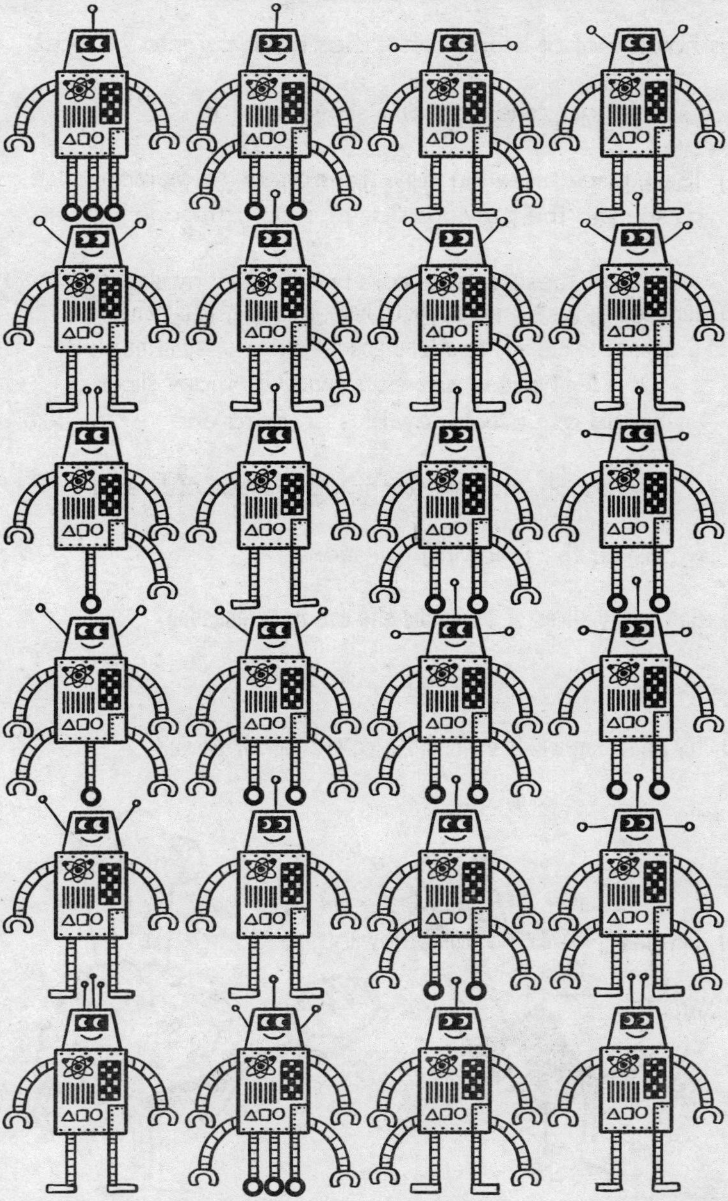

Iris has a loaf of bread, which has been cut into 24 slices.

- On Monday, she eats one slice of bread

- Then, each following day, she eats twice as many slices as she did the previous day plus an extra one:

  So, on Tuesday, she eats twice as many slices of bread as on Monday, plus an extra one

  On Wednesday, she eats twice as many slices of bread as on Tuesday, plus an extra one

  And so on, until she runs out of slices of bread

Now answer the following questions:

a) How many slices of bread did she eat on Wednesday?

....

b) On what day will Iris finish eating the loaf of bread?

....

Can you draw along some of the dashed lines to divide this shape up into four identical pieces, with no unused parts left over?

Each of the four pieces must be identical, although they can be rotated relative to one another.

Take a look at the solved example, to see how it works.

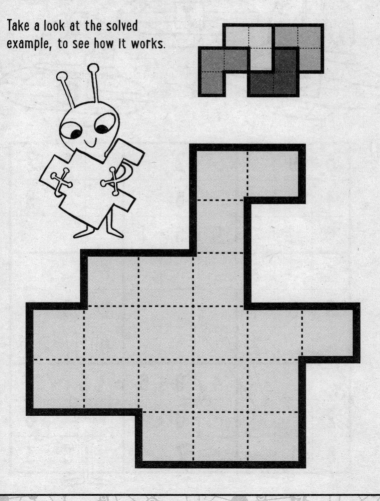

Write a digit from 1 to 9 into each empty square so that no digit repeats in any row, column or bold-lined 3x3 box.

a)

8	9			2			5	7
4				6				9
			9	5	1			
		5				6		
9	8	4				2	3	5
		2				9		
			4	9	6			
2				8				6
6	1			7			8	3

b)

	8		5	2	9		1	
4			3		8			9
		9				3		
1	6			9			3	4
9			2		3			7
2	7			4			9	8
		5				8		
8			9		1			5
	4		8	5	2		7	

If you were to reflect picture a in the mirror then which of the three options, '1' to '3', would appear? Circle the correct option, then repeat for pictures b and c.

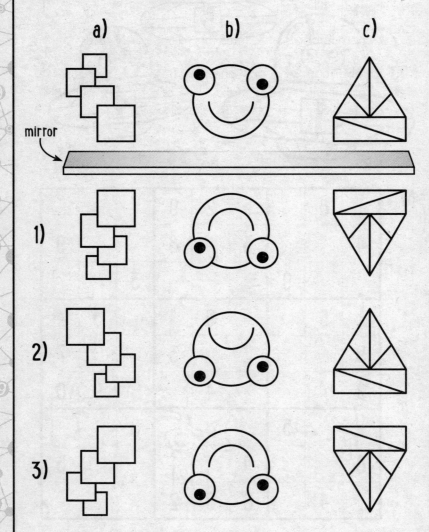

Join all of the following numbers into pairs, so that each pair follows one of these two rules:

- One number is three times the value of the other

- *Or* one number is four times the value of the other

Each number can be in only one pair. Be careful because there are multiple ways to make some of the pairs, but only one way to place them all into pairs all at once.

Draw along the dashed lines to create fences that divide each of these grids into a set of square fields, just like in the example below. Every field must contain exactly one monster, and every grid square must be part of exactly one field.

Here's an example solved puzzle, so you can see how it works:

a)

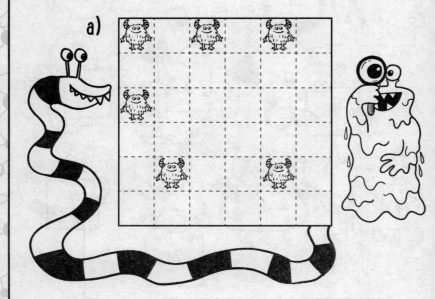

b)

c)

The image at the top of the page has been hidden in one of the four images labelled 'a' to 'd', but which one? The answer must contain the full original image, exactly as shown, but it may have been rotated. Be careful because some of the differences are quite small!

a)

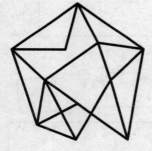

b)

c)

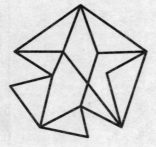

d)

The answer is: ....

Can you find each of these sixteen numbers in the grid?
They can be written in any direction, including diagonally,
and may read forwards or backwards.

100227	292039	579188	739993
115257	420356	677622	900397
166012	442733	69335	913999
215848	458900	725799	957618

7	5	7	3	2	6	3	9	9	9	3	7	6	6
5	7	1	2	2	7	1	5	7	9	3	7	2	7
2	7	0	1	9	6	0	7	5	2	2	2	0	9
5	5	3	3	5	9	6	9	7	9	2	5	5	7
8	3	0	0	2	2	5	8	9	9	6	7	3	5
6	0	9	1	9	1	5	2	1	3	7	9	3	3
9	3	3	6	2	9	7	7	8	0	7	9	7	4
3	2	0	5	8	8	7	8	8	6	6	9	2	3
9	1	2	3	4	7	4	2	1	8	9	6	4	4
5	0	9	0	2	5	9	8	2	6	9	3	4	0
8	6	2	2	1	1	8	2	5	0	7	7	3	1
0	6	2	4	9	1	4	9	3	1	0	5	0	5
6	1	9	7	5	0	0	1	0	8	2	1	9	0
3	9	9	9	3	1	9	1	3	0	8	7	1	6

Imagine looking down on this arrangement of cubes from the direction of the arrow. Which of the options, A to D, would match what you see?

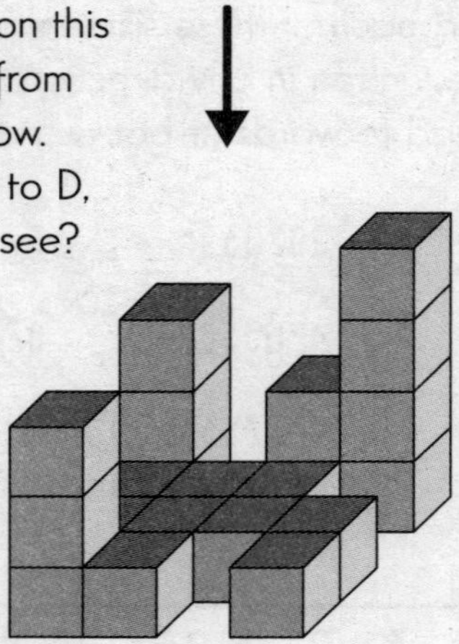

a)

b)

c)

d)

The answer is: ....

Starting on a circle which contains a 1, can you trace a route along the lines to 2, 3, 4 and then 5 in that order, without visiting any number more than once?

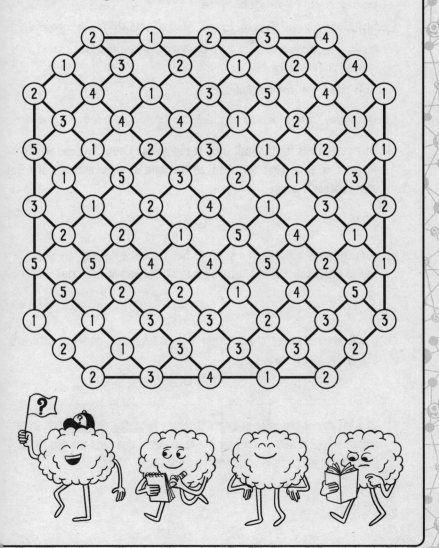

Lucy is visiting some of her family over the summer holidays.

- First she travels from her home to her grandmother's, and spends two nights there.
- She then travels directly to her aunt's, and stays for three nights.
- Next, she travels direct to her great grandmother's and stays for four nights.
- She then returns home.

Each journey from place to place is completed within the same day.

a) How many days in total will Lucy spend away? Count any day where for part or all of that day she is at her aunt's, grandmother's or great grandmother's house.

.... days

b) If Lucy leaves home at the start of her trip on a Monday, on what day of the week will she return home at the end of her trip?

....

c) If she arrives at her grandmother's on 3rd August, on what date will she arrive at her aunt's?

....

d) On what day of the week and date is Lucy's first full day with her great grandmother? A 'full day' means she both starts and ends the day there. Use the day and date information from questions 'b' and 'c'.

Day: ....   Date: ....

Take a good look at this picture, then when you think you will remember it turn the page.

Circle the six changes to the picture. If you can't find them all, check back and forth until you do.

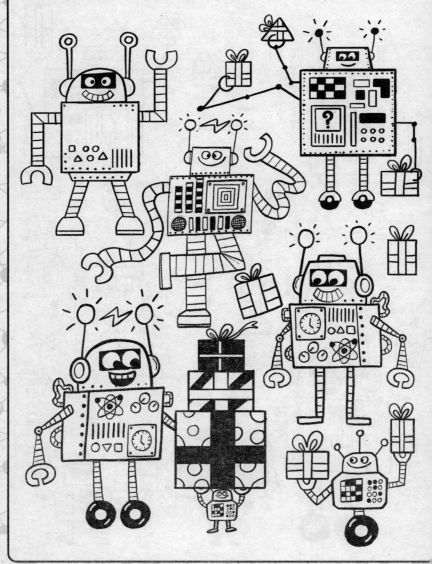

A family has four children: Amy, Ben, Claire and Dan.
You also know that:

- All of the ages are even numbers
- Amy is twice as old as Ben
- Adding Ben and Claire's ages will give you Dan's age
- Dan, aged 10, is the oldest child
- Amy is older than Claire
- None of the children are the same age

Now can you work out how many years old each
child is? Write your answer in the spaces below:

Amy: ....

Ben: ....

Claire: ....

Dan: ....

Some fish are hiding in each of these ponds. Can you find them all?

- None of the fish are in the grid squares with numbers on.

- There is never more than one fish per grid square.

- Numbers reveal the total number of fish in all touching squares – including diagonally touching squares.

Look at this solved puzzle to see how this works:

a)

2	3	2	1
			1
	4	2	

b)

2		2	
	3		2
1			1

c)

	3		2
	3	3	
2			
1		2	1

Draw lines to join each pair of identical shapes, just like in the example solution below. Only one line can enter each square, and lines can't be drawn diagonally.

Here's an example solved puzzle, so you can see how it works:

a)

b)

c)

These eight pictures look similar, but in fact only two of them are identical. All the others have a small difference compared to the rest. Can you draw a path to join the identical pair, then circle the difference on each of the other pictures?

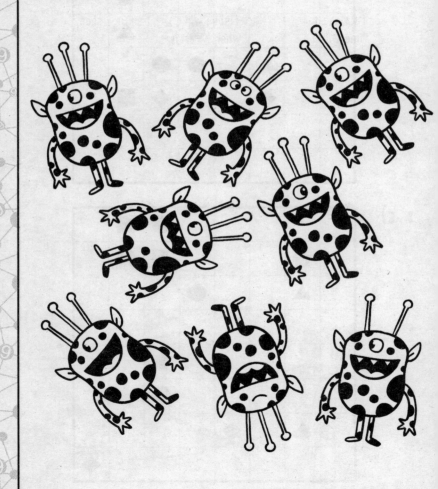

Femi is flying from Lisbon to Seville, and spends exactly one hour in the air on the plane.

Seville's time is one hour ahead of the time in Lisbon, so when it's 10am in Lisbon it's 11am in Seville.

a) If Femi's plane takes off from Lisbon when it's 5pm in Lisbon, what time will it be in Seville when he arrives there?

....

Femi's return flight, back from Seville to Lisbon, also takes one hour.

b) If Femi's plane takes off from Seville when it's 9am in Seville, what time will it be in Lisbon when he arrives there?

....

Write a letter from 'A' to 'H' into each empty square so that no letter repeats in any row or column. Also, identical letters cannot be in touching squares – not even diagonally

Here's an example solved puzzle, so you can see how it works:

G	A	E	C	F	H	D	B
H	C	D	B	G	E	A	F
E	G	F	A	D	C	B	H
D	B	C	H	E	A	F	G
C	H	A	F	B	G	E	D
F	E	B	G	A	D	H	C
B	D	H	E	C	F	G	A
A	F	G	D	H	B	C	E

a)

		G	F	B	E		
	E	H			C	F	
G	F					D	C
A							F
D							B
E	G					C	H
	B	C				G	A
		E	G	C	H		

b)

	B	C			F	H	
D			A	H			G
B							D
	C					F	
	D					E	
H							F
F			E	G			C
	G	F				A	D	

Write a digit from 1 to 9 into each grid square which does not already contain a digit so that no digit repeats in any row, column or bold-lined 3x3 box.

Also, every grid square has been labelled to show what values can fit into it:

- No shape: contains 1, 2 or 3

- Square: contains 4, 5 or 6

- Circle: contains 7, 8 or 9

a)

b)

		○	○				○
○		⑧	⑨		5	4		
	4		○			○	⑦	
	⑧		○		○		3	
		○				○	○	
	⑨				○		1	○
○	6			○	○		4	
		5	2	○	3	⑦		○
○	○						○	

⏱ TIME ....

Take a look at the picture below, which has been drawn using just squares. What is the minimum number of squares you would need to draw to recreate this picture yourself?

.... squares

A mathematical transformation has been hidden in each of these central squares, marked with a '?'. Can you work out what is going on, in each puzzle, to change the circled numbers into the numbers inside the triangles, following the straight-line path of each arrow? For example, in the first puzzle 2 becomes 8 and 11 becomes 44.

a)

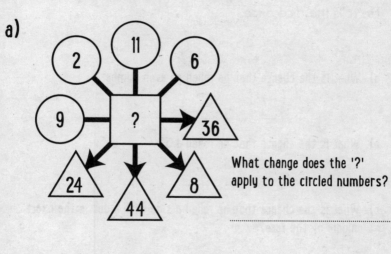

What change does the '?' apply to the circled numbers?

....

b)

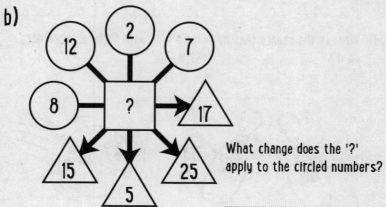

What change does the '?' apply to the circled numbers?

....

Benji has a regular dice with six sides that look like this, corresponding to 1 to 6:

He rolls the dice once.

a) **What is the chance that he rolled an even number?**

....

b) **What is the chance that he rolled a 5?**

....

c) **What is the chance that he rolled a side with a dot in the exact middle of the face?**

....

d) **What is the chance that he rolled a side with three or more dots on it?**

....

These seven pictures might all look the same, but one is slightly different to the others. Can you find and then circle the odd-one-out?

These six tiles can be swapped around to reveal a picture of a number. What is that number? You don't need to rotate any of the tiles.

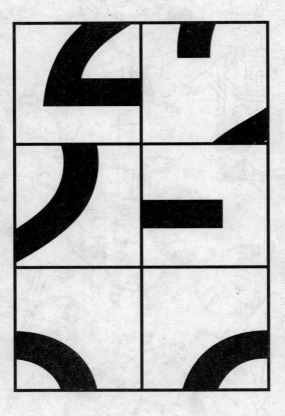

The answer is: ....

All
of the
ANSWERS

BRAIN GAME 1

c) Charlie is 7. This means that Ally is 3 and Bex is 9.

BRAIN GAME 2

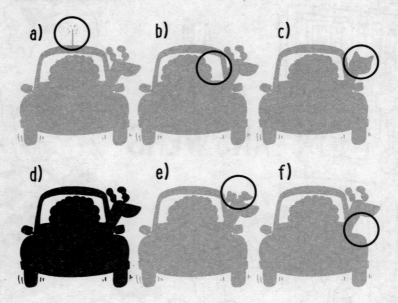

a) b) c)

d) e) f)

The correct silhouette is 'd'.

BRAIN GAME 3

BRAIN GAME 4

a)

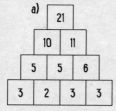

b)

c)

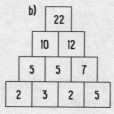

BRAIN GAME 5

BRAIN GAME 6

a) Lottie is travelling in a car
b) Jack is going to Canada
c) Mina is going to Australia

Person	Country	Transport
Lottie	France	Car
Jack	Canada	Plane
Mina	Australia	Boat

BRAIN GAME 7

a) 16
b) 4
c) 2
d) 8 with three antennae (whereas there are only 5 with two open eyes looking away from the centre of the book)
e) 2

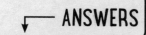
BRAIN GAME 8

BRAIN GAME 9

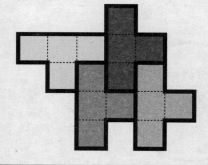

BRAIN GAME 10

There are 7 circles:

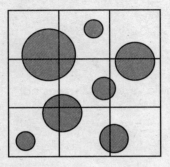

BRAIN GAME 11

BRAIN GAME 12

Cube 'e' is the only possibility.

- Cube 'a' has the wrong face on top
- On cube 'b', the side with the two circles is rotated incorrectly
- Cube 'c' has the wrong face on the front
- Cube 'd' has a face with a single arrow that does not appear on the original picture

BRAIN GAME 13

a) 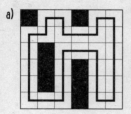 b) 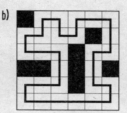 c)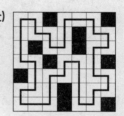

BRAIN GAME 14

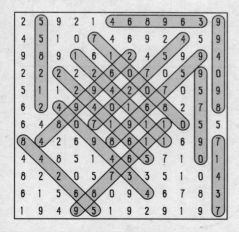

BRAIN GAME 15

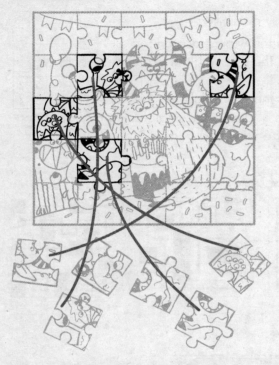

BRAIN GAME 16

a)

	2	🐛
2	🐛	3
	🐛	2

b)

🐛	3	🐛	1
🐛	4	2	
1		🐛	1

c)

1	🐛	3	🐛
2	2		🐛
🐛	2	2	
1	2	🐛	1

BRAIN GAME 17

a)

1	4	2	3	6	5
3	6	5	2	1	4
5	1	3	4	2	6
6	2	4	1	5	3
4	5	1	6	3	2
2	3	6	5	4	1

b)

6	2	4	1	3	5
5	3	1	2	6	4
4	1	5	6	2	3
3	6	2	4	5	1
1	5	6	3	4	2
2	4	3	5	1	6

c)

3	1	4	5	2	6
5	2	6	3	4	1
2	6	5	4	1	3
4	3	1	2	6	5
6	4	3	1	5	2
1	5	2	6	3	4

BRAIN GAME 18

a)

b)
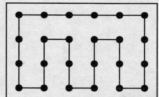

c)
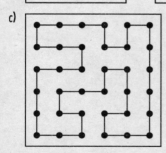

d)
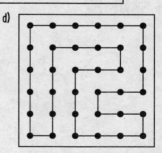

BRAIN GAME 19

a)

A	C	C	A
C	D	B	D
B	C	D	B
D	A	B	A

b)

B	D	A	D
B	A	C	B
C	D	C	A
A	C	B	D

c)

A	D	D	C	A
C	C	A	B	B
D	B	D	A	C
D	B	A	C	B

BRAIN GAME 20

a)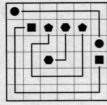

b)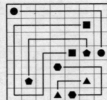

c)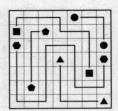

BRAIN GAME 21

a) 1
b) 1
c) 2

BRAIN GAME 22

The two new aliens are:

The two aliens who left are:

BRAIN GAME 23

2	4	7	1		7	1	6	3
9			3		9		2	
4		6	5	9	4	4	5	6
3	1	2		8		2		6
4		1	4	7	9	3		1
3		9		7		3	8	9
7	6	3	9	8	1	9		2
	7		8		1			9
9	4	2	2		4	6	4	7

BRAIN GAME 24

a)

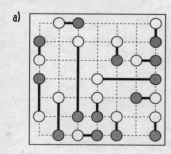

b)

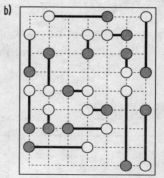

BRAIN GAME 25

The total is 21

BRAIN GAME 26

'a' is the odd one out because it is the only one with six points. All the other stars have five points.

BRAIN GAME 27

a)

B	D	A	E	F	C
A	F	C	B	D	E
E	B	D	F	C	A
D	C	E	A	B	F
F	A	B	C	E	D
C	E	F	D	A	B

b)

C	F	B	E	A	D
E	A	D	C	F	B
D	C	F	B	E	A
B	E	A	D	C	F
A	D	C	F	B	E
F	B	E	A	D	C

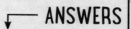

BRAIN GAME 28

a) 3pm
b) 4pm
c) 6pm
d) 4pm – since Los Angeles is 8 hours behind London

BRAIN GAME 29

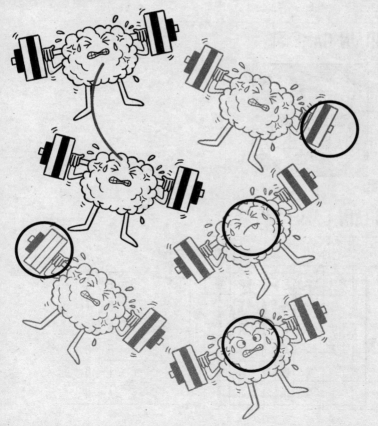

BRAIN GAME 30

a)

D	E	A	C	B
B	A	C	E	D
C	B	D	A	E
A	D	E	B	C
E	C	B	D	A

b)

B	A	C	E	D
C	E	D	B	A
E	D	B	A	C
D	B	A	C	E
A	C	E	D	B

BRAIN GAME 31

c)

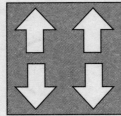

BRAIN GAME 32

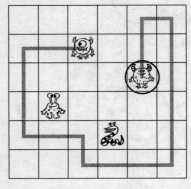

BRAIN GAME 33

The number is '3'

BRAIN GAME 34

c)

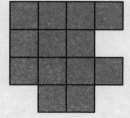

BRAIN GAME 35

a) 14th June
b) Sunday
c) Saturday
d) 24th June

BRAIN GAME 36

There are a total of 11 rectangles.

BRAIN GAME 37

a) 18 bricks: 3 on the top, 6 in the middle and 9 on the bottom.

b) 12 bricks: 2 on the top, 4 in the middle and 6 on the bottom.

BRAIN GAME 38

a)

O	X	X	X	O	X
O	X	X	X	O	X
X	X	X	O	O	O
O	O	O	X	X	O
O	X	O	O	X	X
X	O	X	O	O	X

b)

X	O	O	O	X	O
O	O	X	O	O	O
X	X	O	O	X	X
O	O	X	X	O	X
X	X	O	O	O	X
O	O	O	X	X	X

c)

O	O	X	O	O	X
O	O	X	X	O	X
X	X	X	O	O	O
X	O	O	O	X	X
X	X	O	O	X	X
O	X	X	O	X	O

BRAIN GAME 39

a)

8	6	4	7	3	1	2	5
3	2	1	5	7	6	8	4
5	7	6	2	4	3	1	8
4	1	3	8	2	7	5	6
2	5	7	3	6	8	4	1
6	4	8	1	5	2	3	7
1	3	5	6	8	4	7	2
7	8	2	4	1	5	6	3

b)

4	1	2	5	8	3	7	6
8	6	7	3	5	1	2	4
1	2	3	8	6	5	4	7
6	7	5	4	3	2	8	1
7	3	8	1	4	6	5	2
2	5	4	6	7	8	1	3
5	4	6	2	1	7	3	8
3	8	1	7	2	4	6	5

BRAIN GAME 40

a)  b)  c)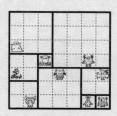

BRAIN GAME 41

a) 9 – add 3 at each step
b) 66 – divide by 2 at each step
c) 67 – subtract 11 at each step
d) 58 – difference increases by 1 at each step (i.e. add 7, then add 8, then add 9, then add 10)
e) 314 – multiply by 3 at each step

BRAIN GAME 42

New monsters:

Monsters who left:

BRAIN GAME 43

4 and 8
7 and 14
11 and 22
16 and 32
18 and 36

BRAIN GAME 44

a)

7+ 3	4 4	5+ 2	4+ 1
4	2 2	1	3
3+ 2	4+ 1	5 3	6+ 4
1	3	4 4	2

b)

6+ 4	2 2	7+ 3	1
2	5+ 4	1	3
5+ 1	7+ 3	4	6+ 2
3	1	2 2	4

c)

4+ 1	3	8+ 2	4
7+ 4	4+ 1	3	3+ 2
3	8+ 2	4	1
8+ 2	4	4+ 1	3

BRAIN GAME 45

All of the shapes are polygons with 6 edges, apart from the shaded shape 'd' which has 7 edges:

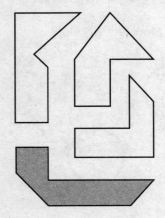

BRAIN GAME 46

17 is the odd number out. It is the only one whose two digits do not add up to 10. For example the digits making up 19 are 1 and 9, and 1 + 9 = 10.

BRAIN GAME 47

a)

B	G	A	C	F	D	E
C	F	E	D	G	A	B
A	D	G	F	B	E	C
E	C	B	A	D	F	G
G	A	F	E	C	B	D
D	E	C	B	A	G	F
F	B	D	G	E	C	A

b)

D	E	B	F	G	C	A
F	C	G	A	E	D	B
A	D	E	B	F	G	C
G	B	F	C	D	A	E
C	A	D	E	B	F	G
B	F	C	G	A	E	D
E	G	A	D	C	B	F

BRAIN GAME 48

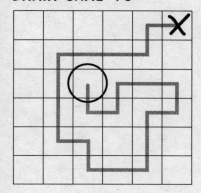

BRAIN GAME 49

How did you do?

BRAIN GAME 50

BRAIN GAME 51

c)

BRAIN GAME 52

Delete the 1 from the 16 to give: 5 + 6 = 11
Delete the 0 from the 10 to give: 1 + 21 = 22
Delete the 1 from the 12 to give: 11 × 2 = 22
Delete the 1 from the 10 to give: 21 + 0 + 5 = 26
Delete either 1 from the 11 to give: 1 + 22 + 33 = 56

BRAIN GAME 53

a)

F	C	B	E	A	D
C	D	F	A	B	E
A	E	D	F	C	B
B	A	C	D	E	F
D	B	E	C	F	A
E	F	A	B	D	C

b)

A	E	B	F	C	D
D	F	C	E	B	A
E	B	D	A	F	C
B	C	F	D	A	E
F	A	E	C	D	B
C	D	A	B	E	F

BRAIN GAME 54

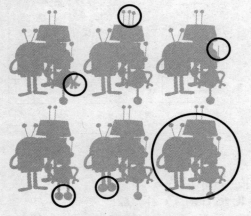

The exact match is image 'f'

BRAIN GAME 55

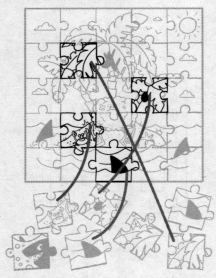

BRAIN GAME 56

a)
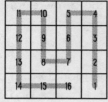

b)
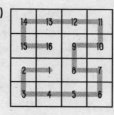

c)
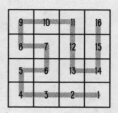

BRAIN GAME 57

8 triangles:

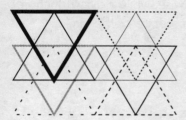

BRAIN GAME 58

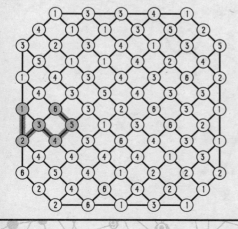

BRAIN GAME 59

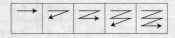

At each stage the arrow extends alternatively straight right or diagonally down and left.

At each step the triangle rotates 90 degrees anticlockwise and one more dot is added beneath it.

At each step the line inside the circle rotates by 135 degrees clockwise, while staying anchored to the centre of the circle.

BRAIN GAME 60

BRAIN GAME 61

'c' is the odd image out because it is the only one where the lines do not cross at right angles.

BRAIN GAME 62

a)

6	9	7	4	8	3	1	5	2
8	3	1	7	2	5	4	6	9
5	2	4	6	9	1	8	3	7
3	1	6	9	7	8	5	2	4
4	7	2	3	5	6	9	8	1
9	5	8	2	1	4	6	7	3
2	8	3	1	6	9	7	4	5
1	4	5	8	3	7	2	9	6
7	6	9	5	4	2	3	1	8

b)

4	2	8	5	6	7	3	1	9
5	6	1	3	9	2	4	8	7
3	7	9	8	1	4	6	5	2
7	3	6	9	2	8	1	4	5
8	9	5	1	4	6	7	2	3
1	4	2	7	5	3	9	6	8
9	8	4	2	3	1	5	7	6
2	1	3	6	7	5	8	9	4
6	5	7	4	8	9	2	3	1

BRAIN GAME 63

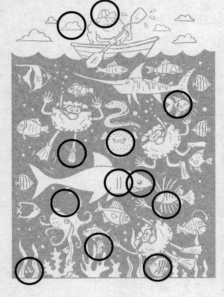

BRAIN GAME 64

7	8	9		8	6	8	1
5		1		7		2	
8	3	4		6		6	6	6
	9	3	5	9	7		5
6	9	6			3	9	3
7		4	4	7	1	9	
1	8	4		6		5	4	4
	1			3		2		2
	5	2	1	2		5	7	3

BRAIN GAME 65

b) Chicken

e) Pig

BRAIN GAME 66

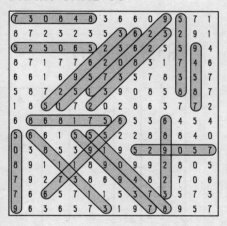

BRAIN GAME 67

a)

3× 3	4	2× 1	2
1	3× 3	8× 2	4× 4
2× 2	1	4	3× 3
8× 4	2	3	1

b)

2	72× 3	4	4× 1
3	2	1	4
4× 4	1	48× 3	2
1	4	2	3× 3

c)

12× 3	1	8× 4	2
4	6× 3	2	1
8× 2	4	1	36× 3
2× 1	2	3	4

BRAIN GAME 68

d) Rashid is three times as likely to pick out an orange ball as a red ball – this is because there are three times as many orange balls (12) as red balls (4).

BRAIN GAME 69

There are a total of 16 rectangles.

BRAIN GAME 70

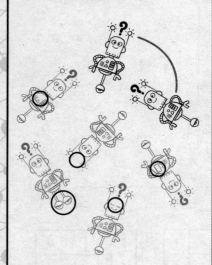

BRAIN GAME 71

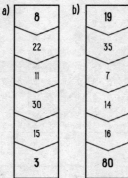

a)
| 8 |
| 22 |
| 11 |
| 30 |
| 15 |
| 3 |

b)
| 19 |
| 35 |
| 7 |
| 14 |
| 16 |
| 80 |

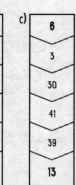

c)
| 6 |
| 3 |
| 30 |
| 41 |
| 39 |
| 13 |

BRAIN GAME 72

a) 36 bricks: 6 on the top, 14 in the middle, and 16 on the bottom.

b) 34 bricks: 3 on the top, 6 in the upper middle, 10 in the lower middle, and 15 on the bottom.

BRAIN GAME 73

d)

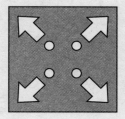

BRAIN GAME 74

Shape 'a'. All of the shapes have exactly one line of symmetry, except for the shaded shape which has two lines of symmetry:

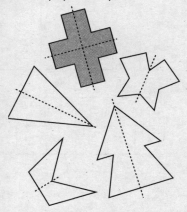

BRAIN GAME 75

a)

3	5	4	1	2	6
1	6	2	3	5	4
2	1	5	6	4	3
6	4	3	5	1	2
4	3	1	2	6	5
5	2	6	4	3	1

b)

2	6	1	5	3	4
4	3	5	2	1	6
6	5	2	3	4	1
1	4	3	6	5	2
5	1	6	4	2	3
3	2	4	1	6	5

c)

2	3	5	6	1	4
6	4	1	2	3	5
4	6	3	5	2	1
1	5	2	4	6	3
5	1	6	3	4	2
3	2	4	1	5	6

BRAIN GAME 76

a)

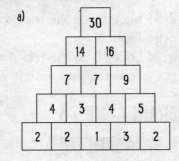

b)

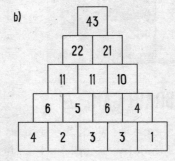

c)

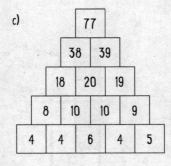

BRAIN GAME 77

a) 11
b) 70
c) 10

d) There are more feet, with 26 feet versus 22 wheels
e) 11
f) 11

BRAIN GAME 78

a) Iris will eat 7 slices of bread on Wednesday
b) Thursday:

On Monday she eats 1 slice
On Tuesday she eats 3 slices (so has eaten 4 overall)
On Wednesday she eats 7 slices (so has eaten 11 overall)
On Thursday she would eat 15 slices – but only has 13 left to eat, so she finishes the loaf

BRAIN GAME 79

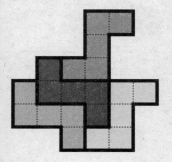

BRAIN GAME 80

a)

8	9	6	3	2	4	1	5	7
4	5	1	7	6	8	3	2	9
7	2	3	9	5	1	8	6	4
1	7	5	2	3	9	6	4	8
9	8	4	6	1	7	2	3	5
3	6	2	8	4	5	9	7	1
5	3	8	4	9	6	7	1	2
2	4	7	1	8	3	5	9	6
6	1	9	5	7	2	4	8	3

b)

3	8	7	5	2	9	4	1	6
4	2	6	3	1	8	7	5	9
5	1	9	4	6	7	3	8	2
1	6	8	7	9	5	2	3	4
9	5	4	2	8	3	1	6	7
2	7	3	1	4	6	5	9	8
7	9	5	6	3	4	8	2	1
8	3	2	9	7	1	6	4	5
6	4	1	8	5	2	9	7	3

BRAIN GAME 81

a) 3
b) 3
c) 1

BRAIN GAME 82

3 and 12 (×4)   7 and 21 (×3)
4 and 16 (×4)   8 and 32 (×4)
6 and 24 (×4)   9 and 27 (×3)

BRAIN GAME 83

a) b) c)

BRAIN GAME 84

d)

BRAIN GAME 85

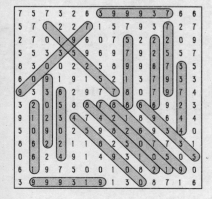

BRAIN GAME 86

c)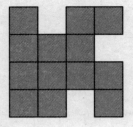

BRAIN GAME 87

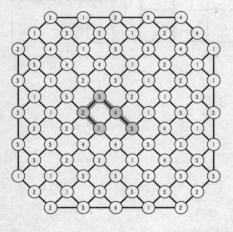

BRAIN GAME 88

a) Ten days – which have nine nights between them
b) Wednesday – which is nine days later than the first day, Monday
c) 5th August
d) Sunday 9th August

BRAIN GAME 89

BRAIN GAME 90

Amy is 8
Ben is 4
Claire is 6
Dan is 10

BRAIN GAME 91

a)
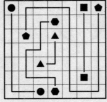

b)
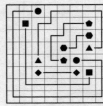

c)
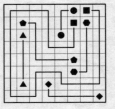

BRAIN GAME 92

a)

b)

c)

BRAIN GAME 93

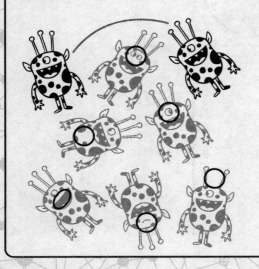

BRAIN GAME 94

a) 7pm – the flight takes one hour, and Seville is also one hour ahead

b) 9am – the flight takes one hour, but Lisbon is an hour behind so he lands at the 'same' time as he took off!

BRAIN GAME 95

a)

C	D	G	F	B	E	H	A
B	E	H	A	D	C	F	G
G	F	B	E	H	A	D	C
A	H	D	C	G	B	E	F
D	C	A	H	E	F	G	B
E	G	F	B	A	D	C	H
H	B	C	D	F	G	A	E
F	A	E	G	C	H	B	D

b)

G	B	C	D	E	F	H	A
D	F	E	A	H	B	C	G
B	H	G	F	C	E	A	D
E	C	A	B	D	G	F	H
A	D	H	G	F	C	E	B
H	E	B	C	A	D	G	F
F	A	D	E	G	H	B	C
C	G	F	H	B	A	D	E

BRAIN GAME 96

a)

8	6	1	5	3	9	4	7	2
3	4	5	2	7	6	1	9	8
2	7	9	1	4	8	5	6	3
9	3	8	6	2	4	7	1	5
1	5	6	3	9	7	8	2	4
7	2	4	8	5	1	6	3	9
6	9	2	4	1	5	3	8	7
5	1	3	7	8	2	9	4	6
4	8	7	9	6	3	2	5	1

b)

6	2	9	1	7	4	3	5	8
7	3	8	9	6	5	4	2	1
5	4	1	8	3	2	9	7	6
1	8	6	7	2	9	5	3	4
3	5	7	6	4	1	8	9	2
2	9	4	3	5	8	6	1	7
8	6	2	5	9	7	1	4	3
4	1	5	2	8	3	7	6	9
9	7	3	4	1	6	2	8	5

BRAIN GAME 97

8 squares:

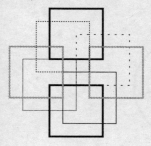

BRAIN GAME 98

a) The '?' multiplies each circled number by 4
b) The '?' multiplies each circled number by 2, then adds 1

BRAIN GAME 99

a) 1 in 2, which is a half. This is because half of the numbers on the dice are even, and the other half are odd.
b) 1 in 6. There is one '5' side out of the 6 sides.
c) 1 in 2, which is a half. Half of the sides have a dot in the middle: 1, 3 and 5.
d) 4 in 6, which is the same as 2 in 3. Four of the six sides have three or more dots: 3, 4, 5 and 6.

BRAIN GAME 100

BRAIN GAME 101

The number is '2'

NOTES
AND
SCRIBBLES

NOTES AND SCRIBBLES →

ALSO AVAILABLE: